To R...
Best!
Harry Warner

A YOUNG LIFE OF LIGHT

A YOUNG LIFE OF LIGHT

By Harry Hathaway Warner

BELLE ISLE BOOKS
www.belleislebooks.com

Copyright 2013 by Harry H. Warner. No portion of this book may be reproduced or transmitted in any form whatsoever without prior written permission from the publisher, except in the case of brief quotations published in articles and reviews.

Printed in the United States

ISBN 978-1-9399300-2-6
Library of Congress Control Number: 2013941009

Published by
BELLE ISLE BOOKS
www.belleislebooks.com

DEDICATION

Of course, to my late grandson, Patrick Gorman; to Breck, Cabell, and Jack Gorman in recognition of their devastating loss and, in spite of its effects, their support in writing this book; to all parents and grandparents who have experienced the same depth of grief from the loss of teenaged boys.

ACKNOWLEDGMENTS

I want to give special thanks to my wife, Sis, for her support and patience; to Sol W. Rawls, Jr. for his encouragement; to Brian D. Shaw for his early support and for introducing me to Rob Walker, who has been not only an editor extraordinaire, but a partner in creating this book.

CONTENTS

Preface ix

Chapter I A Time to Be Born and a Time to Weep 1

Chapter II A Time to Heal and a Time to Laugh 21

Photographs 35

Chapter III A Time to Die and a Time for Mourning . . . 39

Chapter IV A Time to Seek and a Time to Mend 53

Portfolio of Artwork 63

PREFACE

Around the world, thousands of teenaged boys die every day. Some deaths are from natural causes, some from military conflicts, and many are results of immature and misguided behavior such as speeding in a vehicle, being involved with a street gang, getting caught up in drugs, or binge drinking alcohol. Casual observation of the newspapers confirms the frequency of such deaths. Each death is different and each young man is unique. Some attract special coverage because of the notable traits and achievements of the young man in question. Others are reported only in the obituaries. All such deaths, even those of young men who grew up in the worst of life's circumstances, bring a particularly painful grief to the families and friends of the deceased—not only for a life lost, but for one cut off before full bloom. One never contemplates the death of a son and, even more so, a grandson before his own.

This is the story of one such young man, my grandson Patrick Gorman, who died suddenly of latent natural causes at almost eighteen years of age. This story will cover both his life and death. An evaluation of his life is incomplete without consideration of his intangible legacy. Measured against the expanse of human history, his brief existence amounts to little more than a nanosecond, but the lessons his life can teach us are timeless. His life is representative of the will to overcome adversity, the potential for intrinsic human good, the uplifting effect of that good on others, and their equally uplifting response. His is not a testament of fame based on public performance (although he may have achieved that had he lived longer), but is one of quiet appreciation among those who interacted with him. And at that, it was only toward the end and after his life that his peers began to fully recognize his value, as they matured in their empathy, their appreciation for individuality, and their recognition of diversity of talent. Fittingly, it is also a story of miracles.

Since I write as a grandfather, I realize that I must relay this story well enough to convince my readers that it is worth telling on its own merits, and not merely as the therapeutic lamentation of a grieving old man (though it might be this as well). He and I had a particularly close relationship as he was the oldest of my seven grandchildren, and, candidly, I could see some of my genes in him as I could with his mother, who resembles my mother. Of course, I have a vested interest in his legacy, but at age seventy-six, I hope I have the discernment to recognize that he was one of God's best with a story worthy of sharing.

He was fortunate, unlike so many of those described

Preface

at the outset, in that he grew up in a family of Middle American means and with extraordinary love and support. I intend that this book not only celebrate the life of my grandson, but also honor his mother and my daughter, Cabell, her husband, Breck, and their younger son, Jack. Throughout the challenges of Patrick's life, their support of him was unflagging, and their grief afterwards has been unfathomable. Indeed, this is also a story about extraordinarily determined parenting, especially by his mother in her struggle for Patrick's welfare and progress, resulting in her own metamorphosis from timidity into a fighter on his behalf.

This book was written in collaboration with the Gormans, with whom my wife, Sis, and I share such deep sorrow over our grandson's death, although we will never plumb the depths of mourning and depression that they have experienced. Cabell is an accomplished artist in her own right, and it is she who has selected the pictures of his paintings and provided the factual background of his medical, educational, and social challenges. Breck contributed the stories of Patrick's exploits at fishing and shooting, pastimes he taught his son.

This book is intended primarily to perpetuate Patrick's memory among our family, friends, and institutions. At his former schools, I hope recipients of funds set up in his name might read it to learn about him. Perhaps it can inspire young people to be determined to overcome disabilities of one kind or another, to realize that they don't have to be popular to make an impact in life, and to be tolerant of their peers on the premise that there may be more there than meets the eye. The book may also encourage the grieving parents, grandparents, and siblings of youths who have died prematurely. If it unexpectedly finds and is of service to such wider audiences, that is all to the good.

Finally, I write this as a proverbial "labor of love." Tears still come to my eyes when I re-read the many testimonials to Patrick from his peers. It is my hope that you will find his story convincing and uplifting.

Harry Hathaway Warner
November 2012

CHAPTER I

A Time to Be Born
and
A Time to Weep

William Patrick Gorman was born at Henrico Doctors' Hospital in Richmond, Virginia, early on the morning of January 22, 1993, the son of John Breckinridge and Cabell Worthington Warner Gorman. His mother had been in labor for twenty-three hours, and upon birth, his vital signs fell immediately as his lungs were not functioning properly. His dad, who was used to being in operating rooms because of his job selling sophisticated surgical video cameras and scopes, was nevertheless beside himself.

The nurses in the Neo-Natal Intensive Care Unit gave the baby a fifty-fifty chance of surviving. He was placed on both conventional and jet ventilators to breathe for him, requiring a drug-induced paralysis of his lungs. For twenty-seven days—the longest time in the memory of the staff for an infant to be on ventilated oxygen—he remained in that condition. During this time, the ventilators periodically punched holes in his lungs, and his lungs collapsed nine times. The unformed bones in his skull failed to firm up and actually shifted downward due to his lack of movement. There were further complications from the various tubes going into his body, and he lost circulation in one leg, leading the doctors to consider amputation. As Breck and Cabell could not touch him, they taped songs and their speaking voices for him to hear while lying in the crib. He developed *pectus execavatum,* a deep depression of the breastbone often associated with respiratory and cardiac problems, which, in this case, may have been abetted by lungs that would not expand. By all rights, he should have died. The doctors never gave up, but the nurses hinted that he would never be right, even if he survived.

Indicating my grandparental anguish about his situation, I, being a part-time diarist, wrote the following note, which I still possess:

> *I prayed for his life—as many others have—but finally decided that his fate was a matter of God's will.*
> *Also, I realized that if God's will was death, Patrick had already in ten days had a meaningful life—consider the number of people whom he has touched through their prayers for him. And life can truly only be understood through a consideration of and ultimately a confrontation with death.*
> *His suffering has enhanced our contact with God.*

Little did I know that this fateful observation would be even more applicable almost eighteen years later.

Finally, the doctors recommended and asked permission to do a procedure called extracorporeal membrane oxygenation (ECMO), which involves bypassing the lungs and mechanically oxygenating the blood. Although Cabell and Breck were hesitant to give permission because it meant that one of his two carotid arteries would be sacrificed by attaching a valve, there seemed to be no alternative. The doctors set the operation up at Children's Hospital in Washington, D.C., and had a helicopter at the ready to take Patrick that night when they could receive him.

There were prayers from everywhere, and then the first miracle in Patrick's life took place. Shortly before the helicopter was slated to leave, the nurses decided that he was able to come off the ventilator, the operation was canceled, and within forty-eight hours, he was off all life support. Nobody on the medical staff could explain it, and Cabell nicknamed her baby "Angel Boy." He was far from being home free, and he had to stay in the hospital for two more months to address complications of food intake and hydration. All of this took a toll on Cabell and Breck, and, in looking back, she admitted she was naïve about what she was facing.

Baby Patrick came home to round-the-clock nurses working on his feeding and swallowing, plus regular visits by various therapists. Cabell had a "respite nurse" for four hours each day to give her a break. At eight months, they sent him to the eating and swallowing clinic at the Kluge Rehabilitation Center for Children in Charlottesville and took turns staying with him for a month. It is a marvelous facility for children with serious debilitating ailments. Patrick was assigned a team of physicians including a developmental pediatrician, a pulmonologist, and a gastrologist, all from the University of Virginia, to confront his issues. When he returned home, he remained attached to an IV feeding tube first through his nose and then implanted in his stomach. His condition remained touch and go with periodic related illnesses. This routine lasted almost a year.

At about eleven months, he began to say basic words like any infant—"Mama," "Dada," "Boomer" (the dog). Then he came down with respiratory syncytial virus, a serious breathing infection. Back in the hospital in a medicated tent, he was given gentamicin, a strong antibiotic that can be life saving, but unknown to Breck and Cabell, can also cause hearing damage. Some days after his return from intensive care, Patrick began to bang his head against his crib and stopped talking.

Beyond his eating difficulties, clearly something wasn't right with Baby Patrick. Cabell's regular pediatrician thought he had brain damage, and that was the consensus among the physicians in Charlottesville. However, the developmental pediatrician at Kluge wanted to rule out hearing loss and had Patrick tested. He failed in both ears. As devastating as that was, Cabell was relieved. She said,

"I could deal with deafness, but not brain damage." To be certain, he was tested for brain damage with favorable results, and in quick order, they had him fitted with hearing aids.

The medical expenses for Patrick up to this point were extraordinary, and Breck was coming close to hitting the $1 million dollar lifetime cap on his hospitalization insurance through his employer. That forced him to seek new employment to get under a new insurance program. Fortunately, he was able to go to work with a fast-growing national medical equipment manufacturer named Stryker, where he is still employed, but he had to wait six months to be eligible for insurance coverage. He relied on a ninety-day post-employment extension of coverage from his previous employer to help bridge the gap. The family moved to Lexington in the fall of 1994, so that Breck could more easily cover his newly assigned territory of western Virginia.

As if they didn't have enough to endure, on October 5, 1995, Cabell and Breck had another tragedy in their family when they lost a beautiful girl, Frances Nicole, at birth. It was, of course, a heart-wrenching event that added to their stress and sense of the unfairness of life. Offsetting this misfortune, on October 30, 1996, Cabell delivered a normal and healthy boy whom they named John ("Jack") Cabell Gorman. I suspect as I write this he is at football practice at Mills Godwin High School in Richmond.

In their early years, Jack was too young to have

been cognizant of Patrick's travails, though he may have been aware of his brother's special needs and the resulting requirement for parental attention. As with all children, they had different personalities. They had their disagreements as brothers often do. They developed a bond, though, that grew stronger as they grew older, and Jack looked up to Patrick, in spite of his handicaps, for "big brother" counsel and leadership.

Cabell became active in Parent to Parent, a national organization supporting children with health problems, and was also introduced to the state-run Virginia School for the Deaf and Blind (VSDB) in Staunton. After interviews, Patrick was accepted there for pre-school, including transportation, at state expense. Cabell was thrilled to have professionals working with him, shouldering some of the responsibility, because she was exhausted. He attended school there for one year, and while at home, she, Patrick, and Breck worked together to learn American Sign Language.

Over time, through visiting the classes as a volunteer, she began to realize that the VSDB remedial methodology had a bias toward and almost a singular interest in teaching sign language rather than developing speaking skills. (This is not an unusual phenomenon in the close-knit deaf community. I recall reading some years ago about its existence and the surrounding controversy at Gallaudet College, an institution of higher learning for the deaf in Washington, D.C.). Gradually, Patrick was using fewer words and relying less on his hearing aids and more on sign language. Cabell was dedicated to making Patrick as "mainstreamed" as possible, and not having him stereotyped as strictly a deaf person.

Then maybe another miracle took place. I happened to read in the Sunday newspaper supplement *Parade Magazine* an interview with Heather Whitestone, the first totally deaf Miss America, which I clipped and sent to Cabell. Ms. Whitestone spoke about her mother's stern determination that her daughter would not grow up disadvantaged by deafness and would be able to make her way in a hearing world. There was a footnote to the piece recommending that parents of hearing-impaired children contact the Alexander Graham Bell Association for the Deaf. That contact turned out to be a blessing.

The association put Cabell in touch with a Richmond aural habilitation therapist named Pratibha Srinivasan, working under the organizational name Chattering Children, who advised them that there was a limited window of opportunity for Patrick to learn to speak. She recommended stopping sign language "cold turkey" with no coddling. That included moving him to a regular preschool. In her program of "Hear, Listen, Talk!" she stressed maximizing a child's residual hearing. Cabell was hesitant because Patrick was comfortable where he was at VSDB, but her resolve, which was now bolstered by Ms. Whitestone's mother's example, to broaden Patrick's horizon beyond the deaf world kicked in.

Indeed, it was at this point in her life that Cabell went on the offensive. Growing up, she was a wonderful, loving, talented, and bright child, but was somewhat meek and lacked self-assurance. That was mitigated over the years as she matured, went to a boarding school, attended a girls' camp in the summers, succeeded in college in spite of having dyslexia, and got married. Now she turned into a fighter.

Her first battle over Patrick was with the Lexington school system, which, having done an evaluation, wanted to place him in either a handicap class or a Head Start program. Cabell refused and was able to convince them that neither was appropriate. Her plan was to bombard him with individual support and attention and then gradually wean him off to the point where he could compete without aid in a regular school. The school administration acquiesced and agreed to send Patrick to a pre-school, Yellow Brick Road Child Care Center, held at Robert E. Lee Episcopal Church in Lexington. It was the first of many battles with school systems, medical facilities, and doctors that Cabell would win. There seemed always to be variations and conflicts among the many professional medical and educational opinions, and Cabell became adept at sorting though them and taking charge to ensure that her decisions for Patrick be carried out.

Ms. Srinivasan traveled to Lexington to do in-service training for the preschool staff, including reviewing Patrick's audiogram and hearing loss, discussing hearing aids, and explaining the specifics of the job to the aid assigned to him. Simultaneous with Patrick attending the preschool, Cabell paid for and regularly drove him to Richmond to receive auditory-verbal therapy from Ms. Srinivasan at Chattering Children. Ms. Srinivasan recommended that all signing be ceased and offered suggestions as to how to bridge the communication gap. That transition, on top of starting over in a new school with a different regimen, was extremely difficult for Patrick and at first seemed almost hopeless. It took a year for him to progress away from signing back to verbalization. Further, he began to realize that his peers considered him different because of his hearing aids and his inability to hear everything that was going on, particularly in a crowd of exuberant tykes. It began a social challenge that was with him the rest of his life. It is difficult to be on the "in" with children and later with young people when you look strange, with equipment hooked up to your head, and when you can't fully hear. Amazingly, there was only one time a little later in his young life when this overcame Patrick. Cabell and he were in a Costco store, and suddenly Patrick sat down in the aisle and started crying. When she bent down to see what was the matter, he cried, "Why does everybody stare at me?" She sat on the floor with him and they both cried and held each other, completely oblivious to the reactions of those around them.

When Patrick was four, the Gormans moved back to the far West End of Richmond. Not only had Breck's sales territory shifted to the east, but Richmond offered more facilities and opportunities for Patrick's welfare. Again, Cabell had to fight for his best interests by convincing the Henrico County school administration to send him to a private preschool where he had a special aid and the teacher used a microphone that went directly to his hearing aids. Cabell wrote an article in the November/December 1997 issue of *Voices*, a publication of the Alexander Graham Bell Association for the Deaf, describing the adversity that the family had faced and the success that they were beginning to achieve. She said in the article: "I cannot express the feeling I had when I went to pick him up from school, and I saw him playing with other children. I shouted, 'Patrick, it's time to go home,' and he shouted back, 'Not yet, Mom, we're looking for dinosaur bones.'"

To support Cabell and show appreciation to Pratibha Srinivasan for her all-but-miraculous work in shifting Patrick from sign language to speaking almost normally, and to "put something back" into the system, my wife and I, along with all four of our children and their spouses, sponsored a camp for hearing-impaired children over a long weekend in August, 1998. It was held at Camp Mont Shenandoah, a private summer camp for girls in Bath County, Virginia. It is located on beautiful acreage fronting on the pristine Cowpasture River with facilities that are substantial but in keeping with a traditional rustic camping experience. Its regular summer program includes typical girls' team and individual activities, including swimming in the river and a complete equestrian program. About three hundred campers and counselors attend each season.

My daughter, Ann, has been director of the camp since 1996. My wife, Sis, and Ann are the second and third generations of their family to have an ownership interest in the camp. We named the camp session FAIR for Family Auditory Information Retreat, and there were about fifteen families totaling forty parents and children in attendance, all of whom were clients of Ms. Srinivasan's. The session operated on an organized schedule like a mini summer camp and provided an opportunity for those children to enjoy the camp's facilities and country atmosphere—one that most would not otherwise get. It was heartwarming to see the children, including Patrick, all hearing impaired, having so much fun swimming, playing games, and taking hikes, all the while relating so well to each other. The children's parents were encouraged by interfacing with the children in a fun atmosphere and getting to know other parents. When facing a child's disability, nothing is more comforting than participating in a community of families who are all in the same boat. The highlight of the weekend was the same as it was for the regular summer campers at the end of a week—sitting in a big circle before a roaring campfire at a site overlooking the Cowpasture River, with entertainment topped off by several rounds of cooking over the fire and eating "s'mores." The weekend concluded on Sunday with an outdoor church service, more activities, lunch, and departure.

But the Gormans suffered another setback that fall when Patrick's hearing was tested again and the results showed that his hearing loss, for reasons not understood by the doctors, had increased from seventy decibels to one hundred decibels, putting him into the profoundly deaf category. There was now only one option remaining to enable him to hear. Cabell had learned through the Alexander Graham Bell Association about a relatively new device known as a cochlear implant, a microcomputer that is implanted in the skull. The implant converts sound conducted through a small receiver into electrical impulses that stimulate the cochlea, which is the organ in the ear that processes sound. The coded electrical signals bypass the useless cochlear hair cells that normally transmit sounds, and the impulses go directly to the auditory nerve and are interpreted by the brain as sound.

There had been enough of these implant operations performed for us to know that, although not riskless, the procedure posed a low risk of serious complications. Cabell was concerned, however, that in Patrick's case, he had been anesthetized so many times that there was some risk from just putting him under for the operation. At first, he was also skeptical, but he knew that he wanted to hear. So they scheduled the implant procedure for one ear at the Medical College of Virginia in February 1999, a few days after his sixth birthday. We went to Richmond to support Cabell and Breck, and we all waited nervously during the operation. He came through fine and recovered quickly. His head had been shaved for the operation, revealing dramatic stitching, but he brushed it off with his usual sense of acceptance and humor. The only disadvantages of the device were that he had to wear the receiver on his belt with a wire going to a magnetic connector on his scalp to the implant in his head, and that he had to get used to the sounds coming through the implant, which were much less efficient than natural hearing, especially when it came to music and crowded situations. But he could hear! Cabell said that she knew they had made the right decision when some time later they were sitting on their deck and birds were chirping. Patrick asked, "What's that?"

Prior to the operation, Cabell and Breck had been interviewed by a reporter for the *Richmond Times-Dispatch* for a significant article on the front page of the Health & Science section about their journey in attempting to overcome Patrick's hearing problems and the forthcoming insertion of the cochlear implant. In addition to the interview with the Gormans, the write-up included corollary articles on cochlear implants and practical information regarding children's hearing, making it clearly informative and inspirational to other parents with hearing-impaired children.

Entering the first grade at Gayton Elementary School, Patrick continued to have an amplification system used by the teacher, closed-captioned TV, and untimed tests, but he had no aide or special education teacher. Over the next several years, he continued to adapt to and progress in the hearing world and ultimately became one of the first totally deaf children in Henrico County Public Schools to be mainstreamed in regular classes.

When Patrick's mother was a little girl, she was diagnosed as a likely carrier of the gene for Marfan's. Marfan's is a genetic disorder that affects connective tissues and is characterized by the carrier being tall with exceptionally long, thin arms, legs, and fingers. Abraham Lincoln is frequently cited as a prominent example of the physique of one with Marfan's, although I don't think it has ever been proved that he had the condition. It has a range of mild to severe repercussions, including the potential for serious heart, eye, lung, spinal cord, and skeletal problems. My own limbs and fingers are slightly longer than average; however, MRI testing has indicated that neither my wife nor I have any concrete evidence of carrying the gene, and we know of no other case in our family histories. It is possible that Cabell was the one out of four carriers of the Marfan's gene that receive it through spontaneous mutation. We'll never know for sure. However, Patrick clearly had enough of the external and internal characteristics to be diagnosed as having the disease.

His immediate problem was that he had a worsening case of scoliosis, which is a curvature of the spine. Scoliosis is not uncommon, but in his case, by the time he started school, the curvature was so severe from the Marfan's syndrome that his spine was beginning to encroach on his heart. It was clear that he would have to be operated on and have rods, pins, and screws implanted to straighten his backbone and maintain its position. In order to get the best guidance and medical skills, Cabell took Patrick to Johns Hopkins Hospital in Baltimore, where one of the best surgeons in the country for these types of operations was located. His name is Dr. Michael Ain, and he is a story in himself, as he overcame significant challenges to become a renowned surgeon. He is a dwarf, and Cabell and Patrick were taken aback when they first visited him, but he immediately gave Cabell confidence and was uplifting to Patrick when he intimated, "You think *you* have disabilities to deal with?"

The surgery took place on March 3, 2004. Sis and I were there in Baltimore to lend our support, and once again there was great trepidation about Patrick being deeply sedated and going through such a serious operation. He was on the operating table for ten and a half hours as Dr. Ain, who stands on a box to perform surgery, fused not one but two rods into his spine from the bottom of his neck to his tail bone, and took one rib and part of a hip bone to use to fuse the spine from the front. I had the utmost confidence in Dr. Ain, and this was validated when I met him after the procedure and he told me that all had gone well and the operation was successful.

Patrick was in the hospital ten days, and when he returned home, he was home-schooled for two months.

During his recovery, he had difficulty eating, and his weight went down to fifty-six pounds. But Patrick and his parents faced an even more serious problem. Because of the severe pain resulting from the operation, he had been prescribed a drug containing oxycodone, which is a synthesized opiate. Oxycodone and similar prescription painkillers are now the most widely used addictive drugs in the U.S., with more than 15,000 people dying annually from overdoses.

 Cabell and Breck became alarmed about his continued use of the drug and his apparent growing addiction. If Cabell didn't provide it, Patrick would not only experience pain, but would begin to shake violently from withdrawal. She said she felt like a pusher, but her choice was between denying Patrick relief for his acute pain or administering a drug that they knew was leading to a serious problem. As she said, "Where does a mother draw the line?" They consulted the University of Virginia Pain Clinic for guidance and were told that under no circumstance should he go through a "cold turkey" withdrawal. They recommended that he come to the hospital for a controlled reversion process. However, the Gormans knew that with Patrick's medical history, going back in the hospital with intravenous tubes hooked to him for an extended stay would be debilitating. They decided to detox Patrick themselves. They began to reduce his dosage gradually, and then, using a friend's cottage at Gwynn's Island on the Chesapeake Bay for a focused, private change of venue, the two of them, with no outside help, continued the withdrawal process that lasted for a week in total. Although Jack was present, he was not fully cognizant of the seriousness of what was taking place. Fortunately, the weaning endeavor was successful and Patrick emerged drug free. That was of major relief to me because I was aware of the devastating problem oxycodone addiction had become, having read news accounts of its endemic use particularly in southwest Virginia at the time.

Characteristically, as in dealing with his hearing problems, all during the run-up to the operation, all during the recovery period, all during the withdrawal process, and even afterward, Patrick never once complained. When asked how he was doing, his response was always "Fine!" or "Good!" And he always spoke with a smile on his face. He had a scar that ran the entire length of his back, and he would tell people they could look at it for a small fee.

The spinal fusion with the two rods meant that he could not bend except from the waist, and he had to be very careful not to have an accident or forceful bodily contact that would dislodge the rods. Of course, even if he had not been mostly precluded from contact sports before, he now was out of absolute necessity.

In addition to the challenges of Patrick's hearing deficit and scoliosis, Cabell had to contend with two other ongoing health issues throughout his boyhood years. One was that he had to take a daily pill for his Marfan's-affected heart, and, like any kid, he would sometimes blow it off or forget it, so Cabell had to be constantly vigilant that he was taking it. The other was that he was underweight and had sugar imbalances that could and occasionally did trigger hyperglycemia, a condition of high blood sugar that is often benign, but left untreated can have ramifications including kidney, cardiovascular, and neurological damage. When he was in a hyperglycemic state, he would "lose it" and become very difficult. Cabell was so much on his case about eating properly that it became a control issue between mother and son. On the advice of a dietician, she made a deal with him—if he drank sixteen ounces of cream each morning and each night, totaling 2,600 calories, she would let him eat or not as he pleased. This strategy broke the tension between them and worked for several years. Finally, to her relief, when he was about thirteen, he started eating regularly and properly and continued the cream routine on his own.

His final trip to the hospital was not until he was fifteen. A cochlear implant has a lengthy life, but, like any mechanical device, it is limited, and Cabell did not want his implant to expire suddenly, leaving Patrick with no hearing. They mutually decided to insert another implant for his other ear, which would give him hearing in both ears and be a backup for the first implant. That operation was successful, and Patrick had the luxury of hearing in both ears, although it took him some time to acclimate to that.

CHAPTER II

A Time to Heal and a Time to Laugh

Chapter I paints a pretty gruesome picture of the early years of Patrick's life, but it would be misleading and an injustice to him to say that there were not many happy times in spite of his health difficulties. He was skinny, had a concave chest and was deaf, but because of his spirit and demeanor, he was able to enjoy many activities that all boys do—riding his bicycle, swimming, catching a ball, sledding, and so forth. He participated in the Boy Scouts for several years, and also became proficient in indoor rock climbing. We worried that an accident or rough contact could injure him severely, but Cabell and Breck gave him a lot of latitude to be a boy. They also knew, as did we all to a much lesser extent, that he had a dangerous heart condition. He too knew of that fact, but never expressed concern over it or let it hold him back, aside from his obvious inability to participate in contact sports.

One of the first indications to me that he was all-boy came when he had just turned five and was visiting us with his family at Longboat Key, Florida, where we were on our annual three-week getaway in February. On the beach, he had met a little girl named Morgan, who was about his age, and they played together every day. One night while putting him to bed, I was blown away when he looked up at me and in a serious tone asked, "Umpa, is it okay if I kiss Morgan?" How do you answer that from a five year old? I stumbled around and told him that he should ask her first.

A much stronger personal example of his determination not to let his disabilities stand in his way was his attendance at "Camp Umpa." There were three confluent factors that came into play in the creation of Camp Umpa. The first was that when he was a tot and having difficulty with his hearing and speech, he could not quite say "Grandpa" and it came out "Umpa." So that became his official name for me, and then the other six of my grandchildren picked it up. Simultaneously, Cabell wanted to give him an easy-to-say name for Sis and came up with "Too Too." Not only could Patrick handle this name, it is also a sound-bite description of her personality. The name has "gotten legs," as all of our grandchildren and many others both within and outside of our family now call her that.

The second factor was that I have been a fan of camping out since I was a Boy Scout, and have continued it periodically throughout my life. I think it is rewarding to get out of doors and rough it, at least to some extent. The third factor was that until recently, we had the good fortune of living on an eighty-nine-acre farm outside of Lexington with wonderful frontage on the Maury River, including a natural sandy beach, a large swimming area, and many good camping spots.

My grandfather nomenclature, my love of camping, and the farm facilities all came together to create the Camp Umpa concept. Every summer I would spend one-on-one time with each of my grandchildren under the name of Camp Umpa, beginning with camping and going on to other activities as they got older. Not only was the tradition an ideal way to entertain them and spend time with them; it also allowed me to introduce them to camping in the hope that they might catch the bug. So I began with Patrick in the summer of 2000 when he was seven. We swam in the river, cooked over an open fire, and spent the night in our gazebo high on a hill overlooking the river, sleeping on old VMI hayracks and hays (cots and mattresses to non-VMI alumni). I remember the night distinctly because the local high school had fireworks for its graduation, and as it got dark, we could see them plainly from the gazebo. Patrick was enthralled, and I suspect he thought I had the display arranged just for his benefit. Over the next five years, this was followed by camping out on the river beach and in our woods several times, climbing up and camping on the top of Lexington's natural icon, House Mountain, and in 2004, going on a museum tour of Washington, D.C. The House Mountain climb was the most strenuous outing, but he did it with no problems except that I carried his pack part of the way down because his back was aching from his scoliosis. With the success of that climb, I presented to him at the family's summer reunion a certificate making him a "full-fledged member of the Warner Family House Mountain Adventure Club (WFHMAC) by completing the arduous challenge of climbing the face of House Mountain and camping overnight on 'Student Rock' on the top. In so doing, he has demonstrated courage, stamina and a positive attitude, and has become the youngest member of the club." I signed the certificate as "Chief Poobah of the WFHMAC." Since then I have awarded three more such certificates, starting with Jack, and have three more grandchildren to go. This assumes that by the time they are old enough to make the climb I can still make it. I'll be over eighty years old.

The second year of Camp Umpa, when Patrick was eight, lasted a whole week. In addition to camping out for one night on the farm, I had a number of daily activities lined up for him, including art and guitar lessons. Up to that point, there had been no particular indication that Patrick possessed any innate artistic talent. He did draw pictures, like one he did of me in front of the campfire smoking a cigar, with smoke curling around my head. It was a typical, inelegant child's drawing of an impression of something that caught his attention. It was not until age thirteen, when he sent me for Father's Day a pencil drawing of a fish in a stream about to ingest a fishing fly and hook, that I took notice of this potential talent. Even then, I was distracted from the quality of the drawing by the note he wrote on the back: "You are the greatest grandpa ever."

From about twelve years of age on, Patrick's physical health challenges seemed to be coming under control. The Damocles Sword of a weak heart did not change, and though he was monitored closely by a cardiologist, he and his family refused to dwell on the possible ramifications. Of course, he continued to wear the appendages of his cochlear implant, which compounded the usual challenges of maturation and socialization. He had difficulty hearing in groups, which affected his maturity, and his pre and early teen peers thought he was nerdy and goofy. Although I think they accepted him at a distance, they were not willing to take the social risk of getting too close to him, and he had few real buddies. As he got older, they gradually came to appreciate him because of, if nothing else, his warm smile and engaging demeanor. Cabell had coached him that when he was in a group and not able to hear, he should just smile.

Much of his pre and early teen social interaction came through Jack, who was "one of the boys" in his age group and frequently had friends visit the Gorman house. He was and still is an avid player of sports, which I'm sure has abetted his social standing among his peers. Over the years, he has tried football, baseball, wrestling, and lacrosse, finally settling on football and lacrosse as his sports of choice. Patrick was one of his most avid supporters, going to just about all of his games.

To his great credit, Jack never resented Patrick's participation in his group. Nor did he resent the extra attention Patrick received from his parents due to his disabilities and challenges. Early on there had been normal sibling rivalry, but the brothers became best friends as they grew older. When taking trips with their parents, they would appear to outsiders to be close friends rather than brothers, rarely exhibiting the baggage that usually comes with that relationship. I remember when they visited us in Florida when Patrick was about fourteen and Jack was eleven, we bought a two-man inflatable rubber raft in which they entertained themselves in the waves of the Gulf for hours. Cabell has indicated that their family trips are now much more difficult, as Jack doesn't have his best buddy to pal around with. She tries to mitigate that by encouraging Jack to ask a friend, but it's not the same.

Jack has told me that he misses "hanging out" with Patrick terribly. In my wife's and my ongoing deep sympathy for Cabell and Breck's loss, we sometimes forget Jack's loss and the fact that he is going through his own grieving process. Cabell says that sometimes he expresses his grief, but not often. She is, however, acutely aware of the impact of Patrick's death on him.

Jack has told me that he learned valuable lessons through Patrick's example. He appreciated the fact that Patrick never complained about his limitations, made no excuses, expected no breaks, and was determined to live life on his own terms. Jack put it this way: "Patrick showed that complaining doesn't get you anywhere, and if you take a disability as a short cut, it ends up making things worse." Jack has observed other deaf children—some with and some without cochlear implants—who have been mainstreamed through school, and is proud of the fact that Patrick paved the way for them even if they don't realize it.

Indeed, as Patrick grew into a teenager, he exuded an upbeat attitude toward life in general and his own in particular. This optimism was bolstered by a drive to persist and succeed in all areas, much as he had in overcoming his hearing deficiency. Even with the baggage of all of his previous health problems, he entered into what I would call the "golden period" of his life. He was happy, and things were coming together for him.

In April 2007, when he was fourteen, the Alexander Graham Bell Foundation sponsored a seminar in Richmond for doctors, audiologists, and educators. The company that produced cochlear implants invited Patrick to speak about his experience. He performed amazingly well on stage for almost an hour with none other than Heather Whitestone, the former Miss America who had been an unknowing source of encouragement to his mother. He was proud of the picture taken of the two of them, both with engaging smiles.

Under the tutelage of his father, he had, as far back as

age six or seven, developed a love of fishing and became a talented angler as he matured. His dad said that all he had to do was show him the basics and his natural talent took over from there. He was good at reading water and sensing fish. He had natural hand-eye coordination and, maybe because he couldn't compete in contact sports, he was motivated to do well and became competitive. When he was about eleven years old, a new Orvis store opened in a shopping center close to his house. At the opening, they had an artificial stream set up for casting competitions, which involved casting a line with a lure but no hook toward a stone in the water from about twenty yards away. Patrick tried two or three times and then hit the stone. He then got back in line and continued to win a number of gift certificates until I think they told him he couldn't compete any more. Because of his determination, he was hard on himself when he didn't get good fishing results. Breck recalls that on a family trip to Yellowstone National Park, Patrick got very upset when he had bad luck fishing the Blue Ribbon Stream, which is famous for its trout. He recovered the next day when he had better success with cutthroat trout in Yellowstone's Soda Butte Creek.

During this period, the family traveled, sometimes as a result of Breck receiving awards for exceeding his annual sales quota at Stryker. They went to the Dominican Republic, the Grand Canyon, Maine, and various beaches. In addition, Patrick continued to attend Camp Umpa. Over the years, beginning in 2006, we camped out at Douthet State Park and Lake Moomah, bicycled the Virginia Creeper Trail, went to Baltimore with Jack for three nights for Orioles–Yankees games, went to New York City, and worked and played on our farm. I probably enjoyed these times more than he did.

In 2003, Breck, who is a consummate outdoorsman, bought a vacation house for the family fronting on the Piney River deep into the eastern side of the Blue Ridge Mountains. The remote, half-acre property is close to a road but provides considerable privacy. What makes it most enticing is the fast-flowing river and a large deck situated about twelve feet from the water.

The house is good for entertainment as it contains four bedrooms and three baths and has relatively modern amenities. It became a wonderful retreat for the Gormans (and many guests) and a particular Shangri La for Patrick. He called it his heaven and loved to go there, and maybe in an unconscious premonitory sense, he told his parents that he liked the place so much he would like to be buried there. In an un-teenager-like fashion, he would regularly get up early in the mornings to trout fish, and Breck is proud to acknowledge that Patrick became a better fisherman than he and always caught the bigger fish. Jack also enjoyed fishing and the two would often fish together, but he was not into it the way Patrick was. Admittedly they stocked the stream and had an automatic feeder for the fish, but having the fish in the river and catching them are two different things. When visiting there one time, I saw Patrick snag an eighteen-inch trout.

The Piney River house brought the Gormans even closer together (as it did our extended family) and gave the two boys an opportunity to horse around freely. Breck bought motorized dirt bikes for himself and the two boys that they loved to ride on back trails. This added to Cabell's worries about Patrick's vulnerability to a serious accident, but she could not deny him the freedom and joy of riding.

In keeping with their outdoor interests, when Patrick was ten years old, Breck introduced him to the sport of shooting, including target, skeet, trap, and sporting clays. It was more demanding than fishing, and often Patrick would get tired, but over time his spirit of persistence kicked in and he became an accomplished competitive shooter. Here again, Breck said he had natural talent, shooting right-handed although he did everything else left-handed. He had quick reflexes and learned the basics quickly. It also turned out that he had exceptional eyesight (maybe nature's gift as an offset to his other disabilities). On duck hunts, Patrick regularly saw the incoming ducks first and would nail one or two before anybody else even saw them approaching.

In addition to the father–son bonding it enabled, shooting opened up another door for Patrick. Breck thought that because he was such a good shot, Patrick might benefit from being involved in shooting as a team sport. So for about five years, he regularly attended 4-H/NRA shooting-education camps at Holiday Lake 4-H

Educational Center near Appomattox, Virginia, and the Airfield 4-H Center at Wakefield, Virginia. He received a number of certificates of accomplishment and in 2008 qualified for the National Rifle Association's Distinguished Expert rating—the highest it awards. He also completed a hunter education course sponsored by the Virginia Department of Game and Inland Fisheries.

The apex of his shooting experience was when he was fifteen and on the school team that competed in a national tournament in Sparta, Illinois, sponsored by the Scholastic Clay Target Program. Patrick was on the team in trap and sporting clays and shot solo in skeet. Out of all of the teams (representing 1,200 competitors from around the country), his finished in the top twenty. His biggest accomplishment, however, was in a fun competition sponsored by the Beretta Arms Company, called the Annie Oakley Contest, where 221 kids competed individually in shooting trap. They lined up and each got one shot. If he missed, he was out. If he hit, he stayed in for the next round. Patrick finished second!

After that experience, he became burned out on competitive shooting. He was fifteen and getting into the swing of high school, driving his own car, and immersing himself in painting—his true calling. He had enjoyed art and showed some early talent in middle school, but now it became a passion. He carried genes from his mother and grandmother, both of whom have artistic talent. At the time, Cabell was mostly into photography and was taking a class in that as well as one in painting using pastels. She also began to send Patrick to private art classes. He loved art but had not yet found his medium.

The first "oh-my-gosh" moment Sis and I had about his ability was when, at age fourteen, he painted a landscape with a barn, which he gave us and which we hung in a gallery we had in our house at that time. Even I, who cannot draw a stick man and am anything but an art critic or connoisseur, can tell when a fourteen-year-old kid has created something beyond what one would expect for his age. He received several youth art awards, participated in the Congressional Art Competition for High School Students in 2009, and a picture of one of his paintings was published in the Fall 2010 Newsletter of the Virginia Art Education Association.

Cabell and Patrick found that, although they were not painting together, art was bringing them together in a way they had never experienced, particularly during the challenging early years of Patrick's life. In 2006, she built a studio in the attic of her house that provided a space where she and Patrick could paint. They continued not to paint at the same time, as Cabell said they "would be at each other's throats," but gradually they began to critique each other's paintings and to develop their talents together. Cabell gravitated toward painting in oils while Patrick experimented in pencil, charcoal, and acrylic. Both progressed and became each other's best critics. He didn't hesitate to give his opinion about her work, and she said he was always "spot on." Occasionally he would take her advice, also.

He knew he was good, and Cabell, like Breck in fishing, readily acceded to the fact that he was better than she, and was a natural in instinct, proportions, balance, color, and composition. It is interesting to me to note that some of the same characteristics that made Patrick proficient in fishing and shooting, such as excellent eyesight and hand-eye coordination, were assets in his painting as well. He also demonstrated the same type of persistence in his art as in sports. If he created something he wasn't satisfied with, he would start all over. Patrick and Cabell's shared interest in art brought them together in other ways as well. For example, one time when the family was visiting Baltimore, while Breck and Jack went off on their own, Cabell and Patrick spent three hours in the Baltimore Museum of Art, looking particularly at its Henri Matisse exhibit, which is the largest in the world.

Patrick attended Mills Godwin High School in Henrico County west of Richmond, which had an enrollment of 1,900 students—an easy place for a deaf student to get lost—but he was happy and doing well scholastically. Maybe another miracle happened in his life when he became aware of and visited the Center for the Arts (CFA), a special honors program arts school in the county's system. The center, at Henrico High School, is on the other side of town, both literally and figuratively, and Patrick was not enthusiastic at first. Once there, he ran into Carson Jones, a classmate from his elementary school days who, although having attended a different middle school, was now also at Godwin and attending the Center for the Arts in its visual arts program. (The center is a coordinated program with students attending part time there and part time at their home high schools.) Carson convinced him to take another look, and Patrick applied. In a letter of recommendation that accompanied his application, Nancy A. Smith, chair of the county's Hearing Impaired Program, wrote: "Patrick represents an extraordinary example of a deaf student who has far surpassed the limitations that in the past presented life long barriers to educational achievement and professional and vocational success for deaf individuals." She spoke of his talent as an artist, and she wrote, "Patrick's sincerity, dry wit and modest sense of humor are personality characteristics that will endear him to others throughout the Henrico High School campus." He was accepted.

The CFA in many ways was the highlight of his life. Not only was it professional, hands-on, continuous, quality, and focused art instruction, it was a venue where he was surrounded by other kids with comparable talents and ambitions. There were only about eighteen students in his class, and he was able to form deep relationships with them. Carson told me that there was a consensus in the class that Patrick was a talented artist who had a promising future. He further confirmed that Patrick's vision allowed him to pull colors out of what he was seeing and that he had a talent for layering the colors. He used his hands well

Gorman family, 1998: Patrick, Breck, Jack, and Cabell.
Photo by Bruce Parker, *Richmond Times-Dispatch*

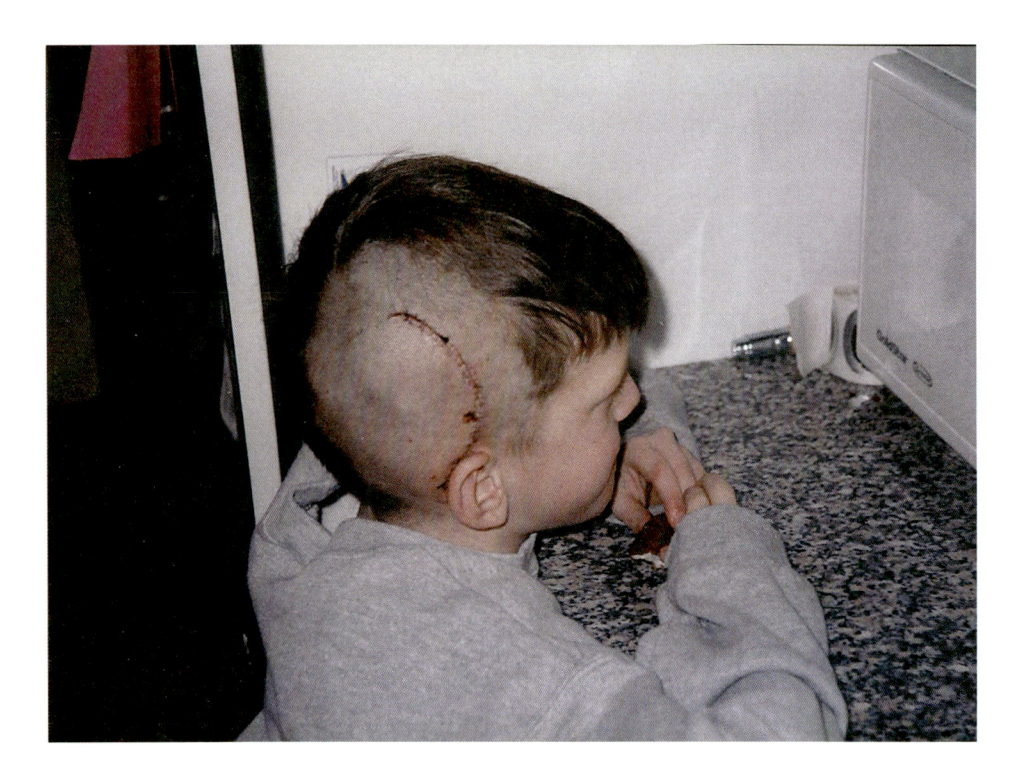

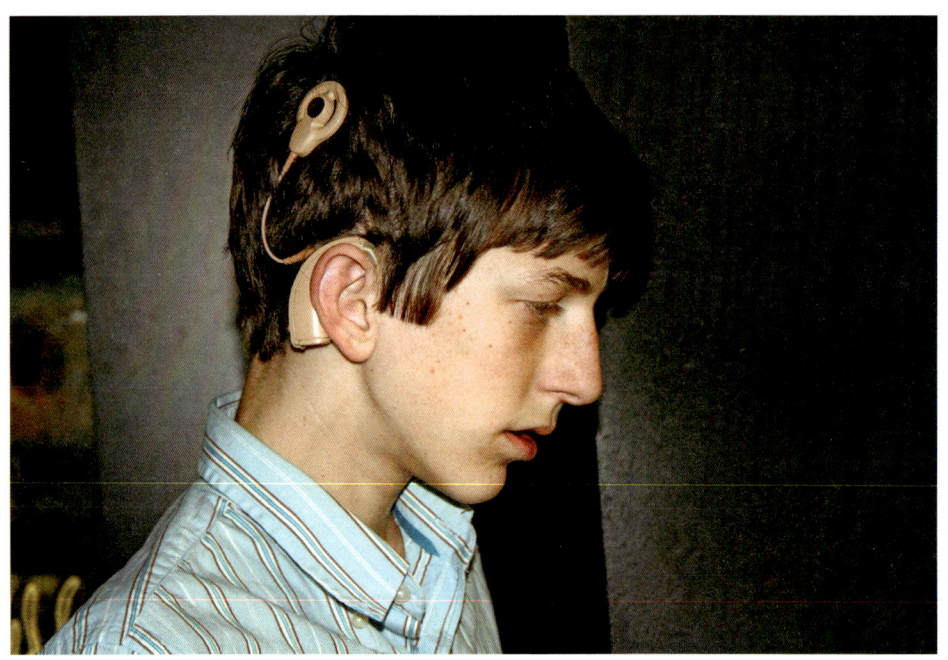

Top: Patrick soon after his cochlear implant operation, with scar from surgery.
Below: The implant as he wore it for many years.

Teaching brother Jack the fine points of fishing on the Piney River.

Two great smiles: Heather Whitestone, the first deaf Miss America, and Patrick.

"Umpa" and Patrick conquer Spy Rock on the Appalachian Trail.

Bring on the competition!

Boyhood pleasure — Cabell's photo of Patrick ran with an article that appeared in the *Richmond Times-Dispatch* shortly after his death.

The pinnacle of Harry's life — Family gathering for Harry and Sis's 50th anniversary at Nags Head, N.C., 2010. From left to right: Ann Batley, Patrick Warner, Ryland Warner, Rebecca Warner, Fox Warner, Sis, Harry, Patrick, Cabell, Breck, Jack, Olivia Warner, Harry Warner, Jr., Hank Warner, Mary Elizabeth Warner.
Photo by PW Photography

and had great patience.

He and Carson became close friends and frequently drove to the Center together, and, according to Carson, did a lot of crazy things that seventeen-year-olds do. At one time when Carson was driving, they were pulled over for speeding 52 mph in a 35 mph limit, and were mistakenly all but shaken down by the police officers for alcohol and drugs. Another time they did wheelies and doughnuts on the muddy baseball field of Henrico High School. These experiences became the same type of teenage lore that I experienced and love to think about sixty years later.

In short, Patrick had finally found his place. He had friends. He had a close buddy. He had respect. He was good at what he did. He was reaching out to girls. He was happy. Although all but tone deaf, he loved to listen to the likes of Jimi Hendrix, the Red Hot Chili Peppers, and Lynyrd Skynyrd. His positive experience at the CFA impacted his life at Godwin, where he participated in Young Life and the Fellowship of Christian Athletes. He was living high school the way it should be.

In the spring of 2010, Cabell and Patrick started to investigate colleges in anticipation of his graduating from high school in 2011. He knew he wanted to major in art, and it was a matter of finding the right college. He was coming so much into his own, Cabell felt he was ready to fly, including going away to school. He narrowed his choices down to Virginia Commonwealth University in Richmond as the safe "home" choice, and the Rochester

Institute for Technology in Rochester, New York, as the riskier home-away-from-home choice. Both were known for their excellent art schools. Patrick and Cabell had a several-day bonding trip together to Rochester to check out the institute, which Patrick liked and was leaning toward as his choice.

In 2010, Patrick had a great summer as he had the freedom of his own car, guys to pal around with, and a job as the head chef (i.e. burger flipper) at the food stand at the Kanawha football fields where his brother played organized football. In September, all of our children sponsored a family celebration of Sis's and my fiftieth anniversary and forthcoming seventy-fifth birthdays by renting several beach cottages at Nags Head, North Carolina. Sis and I went several days early, and were joined by all of our children, spouses, and grandchildren (sixteen in total) for the weekend. It was a perfect family gathering. We had a professional picture taken of all of us walking hand in hand up from the water's edge on the beach, which I now prize as being symbolic of the pinnacle of my life: Being almost seventy-five, but fortunate to have good health; receiving the fruits of raising now-middle-aged children, all of whom were positively engaged in life; enjoying their wonderful children, of whom I was very proud; holding hands with my wife of fifty years and my eldest grandchild, who was preparing for college after years of challenges; in short, feeling extremely blessed. Life would never get any better than it was at the time of the photograph.

Two months later, Cabell, Breck, and the boys visited us for Thanksgiving in Lexington. When they left, I gave Jack and Patrick high fives and hugs, and I remember noting with delight that they were now both much taller then I. It was the last time I would see Patrick alive.

CHAPTER III

A Time to Die
and
A Time for Mourning

I turned seventy-five on Tuesday, November 30, 2010. Although I heard from all of my children and received a present from Sis, the celebration had already taken place at our family gathering at Nags Head in September. It was as much a day of reflection as one of celebration.

That night I was sound asleep when at about 11 p.m., I heard a pounding on the bedroom door and my son Harry Jr. shouting at me to open the door and come downstairs immediately. He had already set the alarm off, and, as he later told me, he knew I had guns in my room and wanted to make sure I knew who it was. I remember thinking that he and maybe my other children were playing a birthday joke on me.

When I got downstairs, Sis, having heard the alarm, was already there, as were our son Patrick and daughter Ann. They immediately told us that young Patrick had died earlier that evening. Sis, who had instinctively known that something was terribly wrong, collapsed to the floor, and I went into a state of shock. It was the worst moment of my life.

The children stayed for the night, built a fire in the fireplace, and stayed up until about 2 A.M., consoling Sis. I had to have some time to myself, so I went back to bed and lay there wide awake in a state of traumatic grieving for the rest of the night. We will be forever grateful to the three children for traveling from Richmond and Bath County to tell us the news so we wouldn't get it over the telephone, and then for staying there with us.

I don't know how many birthdays I have left, and it doesn't matter. November 30 is no longer my birthday—it is the date of Patrick's death and always will be. Cabell is convinced, and I like to believe, that because Patrick and I were so close, there is cosmic significance to the fact that he died on that day. I don't know that God pulls the strings to that extent, but there may have been a spiritual force at work in this case beyond mere coincidence.

That afternoon in Richmond, at about 6 P.M., Jack had been upstairs with his mom in their home, when they heard a loud thud downstairs. Cabell told Jack to go down and see what it was. He screamed back to her that Patrick was lying on the floor not moving and didn't seem to be kidding. She rushed down and I think knew immediately in her heart that Patrick was dead. She said that she saw his spirit rise from his body while he lay on the floor. As they frantically called 911, Breck walked in from work.

They tried to resuscitate Patrick, and the medics, who were there in minutes, worked on him forcefully there and as they rushed him in the ambulance to the Henrico Doctors' Hospital. Cabell also went in the ambulance, saying, "I have been with him all his life—I'm not leaving him now." Breck and Jack followed in the car.

Cabell had called her brother Patrick, a Richmond policeman, who was in the process of picking up his own children. He was at the hospital in minutes and was present when the doctor announced that Patrick had died immediately from an aortic dissection. He in turn called his brother Harry, and they stayed with Breck and Jack at the hospital. Shortly after that, they left to come to Lexington, called Ann from the car, and met to come to our house.

The next morning we drove to Richmond and found Breck, Cabell, and Jack in a state of complete despair. Nobody could stop crying. Breck was so distraught that he told me that he wanted to die. Even living with the knowledge that a defective heart could take Patrick's life at any time did not prepare the family for the stomach-turning shock of his death.

That afternoon, to express my feelings and to allay my grief, I turned to writing. With tears welling up, I sat on their front porch and composed a eulogy, which I thought I could read at his funeral. Later I realized that I could never get through it and asked Harry Jr. to read it, which he would do with steadiness. In the afternoon, the entire family went to the funeral home to view the body, which Cabell, Breck, and Jack endured only because they were so traumatized that they were numb. With that said, however, they had the courage and presence of mind to donate Patrick's eyes to the Old Dominion Eye Foundation. He had designated that on his driver's license. Given the quality of his vision, I'm sure the gift was a blessing for the recipient.

That night a wonderful thing happened that was the first indication of an amazing and virtually unknown truth about Patrick that even his family didn't fully comprehend. We were all in the Gorman house and became aware of a commotion going on in the front yard. To our amazement, we looked outside to see young people carrying lighted candles in a silent vigil in memory of Patrick. They filled the front yard and spilled out onto the street. I was told that the number grew to five hundred. The family gathered on the front porch and tried to take in the significance of what was unfolding in front of us: here was this active outpouring of mourning for a boy who supposedly had few close friends and who was sometimes snubbed by his peers. The kids stood there in silence for about a half hour until Breck made a statement of appreciation to them. Then dozens of them came up to the porch to deposit individual testimonies and condolences about Patrick, written or scribbled on small pieces of paper, sympathy cards, three-ring-binder paper, and formal notecards probably provided by the organizers of the vigil. About a hundred missives were placed on the porch. The sentiments were personal and impromptu, but they expressed common themes about Patrick:

He was always filled with joy and happiness. I cannot imagine going through what he has. He made the best of what he was given every day . . .

Thanks Patrick for being my friend when no one else would be. I'll never forget you.

Patrick was a gift to the world and he will be missed.

Those gathered finally began to disperse, although small knots of them lingered, talking quietly amongst themselves. We were all surprised and deeply appreciative. Such vigils are not uncommon in the case of teenage deaths, but most reflect the shock of loss from car accidents or drug-related incidents and/or recognize a youth who was a popular athlete or school leader. Given Patrick's less attention-drawing natural death, his ostensible detachment from his peers, and the fact that he was certainly not an athlete or leader, one could attribute the vigil turnout to a general sense of loss for one of their age group and a dutiful obligation to acknowledge his death. There may have been some of that, but the size and behavior of the group seemed to reflect a genuine and personal sadness for the loss of one of their own who meant more to them than met the eye. The many notes left behind were moving personal testimonies about Patrick and how much the writers thought of him. Patrick would have been amazed at the whole spectacle.

As is often the case, the affairs of the world intrude on one's life, and the next day, Sis and I had to return to Lexington to sign the contract for the sale of our farm to Washington and Lee University and for me to do some business in Staunton regarding the estate of my brother, who had just died in October. Breck wrote an obituary for Patrick, which appeared in the *Richmond Times-Dispatch* on December 3, and family and friends helped make arrangements for the funeral on Saturday and a reception for out-of-town attendees on Friday night.

The reception was held in a hotel near the Gorman residence with members of the extended family and many close friends attending. The mood was somber but was somewhat alleviated by family and friends reconnecting with others they had not seen for some time. There were displays of Patrick's art and photographs of him provided by members of the family. Cabell and Breck, still in shock, put on brave faces but departed early.

The funeral was held the next day at the Gorman family's church—Christ Episcopal Church—with the Reverend Paul A. Johnson officiating and the Reverend Hillary T. West assisting. The church was packed, with over three hundred people in attendance. Many of Patrick's contemporaries were present, and friends and supporters of the Gormans and ours came from Lexington and other parts of the state. Reverend Johnson gave a wonderful homily, and among other things that captured Patrick, he had this to say:

> *The Apostle Paul wrote that suffering produces endurance; and endurance produces character; and character produces hope . . . his way of saying that the fruit born of challenge is greater than the fruit born of ease. Patrick bore fruit; and I can witness to you that he knew not just hope, but faith. You see, you need to know there's a message of hope and faith from Patrick embedded in this worship service today. It's another gift he gave . . . . Just recently, Patrick and his father had been talking about what kind of senior quote to put in the senior yearbook. " . . . Whatever you ask in prayer, believe that you have received it, and it shall be yours" is what he chose.*

Several nights later, I woke up in the wee hours with a knot of lament in my stomach, but with the sense that I had to start dealing with Patrick's death. As is so often the case, I turned to writing and sketched out a poem. It is doggerel, but it was therapeutic for me.

So at death began the revelation of the extent of the light that had emanated from Patrick during his short life. We knew he was special, but we didn't know how many people he had touched, and I suspect neither did he. He went about his life quietly interacting with others without being overtly upset when they did not respond in kind. He wasn't aware that his smile, his friendly demeanor, and his low-key but obvious commitment to overcome his handicaps were registering with and providing a powerful example for many with whom he came in contact. He knew he had artistic talent, but I don't think he knew how much it was appreciated.

This discovery continued and was enhanced in the months following his funeral by an outpouring of reporting in newspapers about his life and death. First, there was a long, front-page article and picture in the *Richmond Times-Dispatch* just days after his funeral. The Godwin High School newspaper, *The Eagles Eyrie*, carried a feature article on him on December 10. This was followed by an article in the *Lexington New-Gazette* on December 22.

As indicated in the Godwin article, "a giant graffiti wall" was placed opposite the school's main office for students to write messages in honor of Patrick. It turned out to be four three-feet by six-feet pieces of paper with about 360 messages and signatures, which were later given to Breck and Cabell. The teachers and the entire student body of the visual arts department at the Henrico Center for the Arts each painted or drew five-by-seven-inch pictures of their own creation in memory of Patrick, which also were presented to Breck and Cabell.

Virginia Wildlife magazine, in its April 2011 issue,

featured one of Patrick's paintings, a fisherman's hand holding a fishing rod and a colorful Brook Trout, on its cover. The painting was titled, "Beautiful Brookie," and the inside cover acknowledgement said, "This issue of *Virginia Wildlife* is dedicated to the spirit of fly fishermen everywhere; and especially to cover artist W. Patrick Gorman, whose love of the outdoors and vibrant paintings uplifted all who knew him." A copy of the cover is among those paintings in his representative portfolio at the end of this book.

The Center for the Arts established the William Patrick Gorman Memorial Fund in memory of Patrick. Students and faculty made the initial donations, which endowed awards to visual-arts students to pay for things like travel and supplies.

At the time of this writing, the fund, which is held by the Richmond Community Foundation, has a balance of close to $20,000. The contributions have come from many sources. The health and physical education department at Godwin High School contributed $2,000 to a memorial award "in tribute to Patrick's spirit." This was announced at the senior class awards program on June 9, 2011, which we attended with Breck, Cabell, and Jack. At the baccalaureate service on June 14, Breck and Cabell were invited to make comments, but were overwhelmed emotionally by the prospect and asked Patrick's friend Carson Jones to read a letter from them instead. At the June 15 graduation, they were asked to receive Patrick's diploma, the first to be handed out, but again asked Carson to fill in for them. They were informed that Patrick had been slated to graduate with honors.

On May 7, the Center for the Arts opened its 2011 Senior Show, which was dedicated to Patrick. The invitation to the opening reception was a copy of a creative and colorful composite portrait of him—a montage (featured on the cover of this book) to which each of his classmates had contributed a piece to be fitted into the whole. As one entered the venue for the show, there was a representative presentation of his art on the wall, along with an attached description of the students' affection for him and an explanation of how the composite picture of him was created. During the reception, Carson Jones gave a short speech about Patrick, and the principal, Dr. Stephanie Poxon, unveiled a memorial plaque to be displayed permanently at the school, describing the awards endowment in his memory. The plaque reads:

In Memory of William Patrick Gorman
1993 – 2010
In Honor of Our Beloved Student, Classmate and Friend
"Art is not what you see, but what you make others see."
–Degas

Finally, an article and photograph ran in the September 9, 2011, *Farmville* (Virginia) *Herald*, announcing the first annual Patrick Gorman Memorial Scholarship at the 4-H

Shooting Camp. It had been funded initially by Patrick's shooting coaches by passing the hat at a meeting. Our expectation is that the coaches and others will continue to fund the award so that it can be presented each year.

The months succeeding Patrick's death have not been kind to any of us. Sis and I think of him frequently at odd times. We would be proud to be watching his progress through college. But our mental state pales to that of Cabell and Breck. They both have struggled, and I know there are days when Cabell finds it hard to get out of bed. At one point, she wrote me a note that said, "My heart is breaking. I will have to find a way to move forward." Her loss was not only of a son, but of one whose survival and welfare she had fought for his whole life—one who had miraculously blossomed into her artistic partner and soul mate. It is hard enough to lose a grandson, but it is almost unbearable to watch Breck and Cabell trying to deal with their grief. I have a classmate from VMI who, about thirty years ago, lost a son just a little older than Patrick. He told me that it took his wife and him many years to get back into a normal life and that he would never get over the loss.

On May 7, 2011, Cabell had a small, family-attended burial at their place at Piney River. She and Breck had found a way to accede to Patrick's expressed desire to be buried there, as there is a small, out-of-the-way country cemetery not more than a half-mile from their house. It is in a delightful, peaceful, hidden setting, part of the way up a mountain, surrounded by trees and overlooking the Piney River—a perfect place for Patrick's ashes. We gathered, walked to the cemetery in silence, and had a brief interment ceremony conducted by our good friend, Reverend R. David Cox, who, among the many services he has performed for our family, married Breck and Cabell. It was a beautiful sunny day in the mountains where the leaves on the trees still had the light green of early spring. Afterward, Cabell hosted a luncheon at their house, where the grandchildren had a great time playing and the adults sat on the deck overlooking the river. It was especially hard for Breck and Cabell, but both made it through the day with courage.

Cabell has placed a bench in front of Patrick's tombstone, which has engraved on it his name, dates of life, and the words "Fly Away Sweet Angel." The inscription was taken from a song that he liked, "Fly on My Sweet Angel," by Jimi Hendrix, and perfectly depicts his family's remembrance of him. Any time she goes to their Piney River house, Cabell spends time sitting on the bench in silent grief. On the day prior to the first anniversary of his death, Sis and I went to the Piney, planted some winter greenery and daffodil bulbs, and put a Christmas wreath on his grave. I had a little hint of what Cabell goes through when Sis gave me about twenty minutes by myself on the bench. It was a tough, poignant time. I felt a deep sense of loss.

CHAPTER IV

A Time to Seek
and
A Time to Mend

As I write, Breck and Cabell continue to make every effort to find a new normal, but it remains difficult. They are spending a lot of time and attention on Jack as he deals with the loss of his brother and finds his own way through his mid teens. They avoid social events, particularly those connected to holidays. Breck made his Stryker sales quota for 2011 and is on target for 2012, but does not seem to have the same "fire in his belly" for getting up and hitting it every day. He continues to find escape in fishing, hunting, and shooting. Cabell has confided in me that she is a different person with a much different outlook on life and what is important. She has completed a yearlong program to become a docent for the Virginia Museum of Fine Arts and has gotten back to her own painting. She has decided to concentrate on portraits of dogs on a commission basis, combining her love of them with her love of painting. I think she has found a great niche, as last winter she had a two-month exhibit at the University of Virginia Main Hospital where she sold a number of the paintings, and is generating multiple ongoing commissions.

Young Jack has had his own difficulties in dealing with his brother's death. Being so well connected to friends and so involved in sports and school, it is not readily apparent, but his mother has disclosed to me that he still has down days thinking of Patrick. He has turned sixteen and "graduated" from Camp Umpa. Beginning with this past summer, I now rely on him for muscle and leadership at my camp for his seven- eight- and nine-year-old male cousins, and have entered into a "contract" for his services for the next few years in exchange for giving him my 1999 Chevrolet Silverado truck.

Although the mending process for the whole family will be long and arduous, I have every confidence that they will get their lives back on course over time.

I have tried to focus on how fortunate we were to have Patrick with us as long as we did, and I think fondly of the times we had together. I also am grateful for my other six grandchildren—Jack, Olivia, Mary Elizabeth, Fox, Hank, and Ryland. Patrick's death is hard to accept, but what was articulated in wisdom beyond his years by one of his teenaged mourners rings true to me: "Death exists, not as the opposite, but as a part of life." Further, his life was a series of miracles, and I think a clear case can be made that a short life of challenge and significance is superior to a long one of dullness and meaninglessness.

Setting aside these personal feelings, here is the question: Is there anything remarkable about Patrick's life beyond that he was a young man much loved by his family, that he was confronted with challenges all of his life, and that he had an unfortunate and premature death? As I said earlier, thousands of young men die every day, some having demonstrated particular talents during fruitful short lives, and all leaving behind high levels of grief. What makes Patrick's case special?

He was not a genius. He clearly had artistic talent, but, without the opportunity to develop it, we'll never know how much. It is also clear that he endured considerable hardships, especially in his formative years, that he was brave in the face of them, and never complained about them or let them become an excuse. These qualities made Patrick exceptional, but others have dealt with equal or greater handicaps in a manner that made them equally exceptional.

Patrick, however, was blessed with a high quotient of two characteristics that I believe elevated him from exceptional to the realm of extraordinary. One was tenacity. In his drive to overcome his physical limitations, particularly his hearing, and to excel in schoolwork, fishing, shooting, and art, he exhibited dogged determination. For example, he said in his college applications describing himself:

> *Deafness has affected me every day of my life. Every conversation, every teacher's lecture, every time I try to express my thoughts, I have to try so much harder just to be average. It has given me some difficulties in school as well as my social life.... Nobody knows how hard I have worked.*

Just as he didn't complain about his challenges, he didn't speak about his resolve. Even in boyhood, he was a natural example of the lesson from one of my favorite quotations:

> *Press On*
> *Nothing in the world can take the place of persistence. Talent will not; nothing is more common than unsuccessful men with talent. Genius will not; unrewarded genius is almost a proverb. Education alone will not; the world is full of educated derelicts. Persistence and determination alone are omnipotent.*
> *— Calvin Coolidge*

The second and more important gift, which I am convinced enhanced Patrick's uniqueness, is that he possessed an understated spirit that had a positive and uplifting effect on others. On November 28, 2010, at 12:45 p.m., two days before his death, he posted his last entry on Facebook. It was simply ":)". I am not a Facebook aficionado and know nothing about its language. I am told, however, that :) means "smiley face." It was Patrick's way of telling the world simply that he was happy and that he wished the same for everyone else.

I suspect Patrick had little idea of the ways his spirit affected others. His good nature was not contrived, but a natural characteristic—probably partially genetic but certainly honed by his childhood difficulties. After his death, it really became clear that he'd had a significant impact on the people around him. Beginning at 10:53 P.M. the night of his death, the first entry about Patrick was posted on Facebook:

> *That day you told that story about what you've been through in life made me cry like a baby. I know you're up with the big man upstairs and I just want you to know that you've touched a lot of lives, including mine and I wish I could have told you that before you left man. I know you'll be watching over us bud. Take care.*

That set the theme of hundreds Facebook posts, mostly from his peers, over the next two months. Around the time of his eighteenth birthday, almost two months later, there were an additional 113 postings. After that, my son Patrick ceased keeping a record, but here is the amazing thing: In preparation for writing this book, Cabell and Jack went on Patrick's Facebook page for me and found a number of postings from his classmates expressing sadness that he was not at his high school graduation and surrounding events in late May and early June 2011, five months after his death. For example:

What an incredible moment tonight at the senior awards assembly, look at you still making people move (:

Patrick, the senior class gave you a standing ovation last night at the senior awards assembly. Thinking about you.

Then, even though his high school classmates were spread to the winds in college and at work, periodic postings continued. Around the first anniversary of his death, there were forty-six postings acknowledging the day, such as:

One year ago I lost one of my oldest friends. I still miss him everyday [sic] and so does everyone else that knew him. Patrick Gorman, you have no idea how many lives you've touched and I miss you and love you.

> *I can't believe you have been gone for a year. You are missed by so many and so many people look up to you. I know I do. Thank you for being my inspiration. We miss you and know you are looking over us.*

Amazingly, on his nineteenth birthday on January 22, 2012, almost fourteen months after his death, he continued to be memorialized as postings increased, although to make an entry, one had to search for his expired Facebook page and know that because of the expiration, the posting would go nowhere else. These later postings were simply personal and private outreaches to Patrick. The Facebook record is in keeping with the spontaneous outpouring of tributes that began at the candlelight vigil the night after his death.

What is the measure of a life well lived? Contrary to the fixation in modern medical science and society on prolonging life, it is not its length. Nor obviously is it all about the cliché of success in the conventional sense of fame or fortune. Without trying to sermonize, I would say that it is the measure of one's contributions to and effect on others that really counts. In his short life, Patrick left such an enduring legacy—one greater than some who live the proverbial three score and ten or more. His uncle Patrick put it this way: "He was never going to be the most popular or the class president or the valedictorian, but he had more of an impact on those around him than they did combined."

A Young Life of Light

Throughout recorded history, many spiritualists and thinkers from disparate times and places have equated human consciousness and exceptional spirit to light that emanates from the Creator. For example:

The one "I am" at the heart of all creation,
Thou art the light of life.
  —Shvetashvatara Upanishad

. . . the self-originated Clear Light, eternally unborn
. . . shining forth within one's own mind.
  —The Tibetan Book
    of the Great Liberation

God is the light of Heaven and of the Earth.
  —Quran

Time and space are but physiological colors
which the eye makes. But the soul is light.
  —Ralph Waldo Emerson

With all your science can you tell how it is,
and whence it is, that light comes into the soul?
  —Henry David Thoreau

No follower of mine shall wander in the dark;
he shall have the light of life.
  —Jesus Christ (John 8:12)

Patrick, to my knowledge, never demonstrated a deep commitment to formal religion (not unusual for one his age), but I can't help but think that his spirituality was derived from the Light of God. With all his problems, he had an innate sense of peace and inner strength, always accompanied by a smile, which he could not have garnered from the secular world at his age and level of experience. One major indication of this underlying spirituality was that some months before his death, he drew a pencil sketch of the crucified Jesus Christ. Cabell discovered after his death that at some point after completing the drawing he wrote at the top:

> *The closer to death, the closer we are*
> *to comprehend how astounding life is.*
> *The value of life is the most desirous*
> *thing we own.*
> *Don't waste it.*

Not only was that insightful for a seventeen-year-old, it may have been a premonition regarding his own coming death—a possibility of which he was aware, but from all appearances did not focus on or fear.

Patrick was right. In the final analysis, all any of us is given is a chance to live. Scientists and spiritualists argue about the extent to which we are only products of nature and nurture. However, we know from observation that the lives of individuals come in all shades and that occasionally someone comes along who casts a light for others. Patrick was true to his own dictum of not wasting his life. More significantly, to others, his was a bright but tragically brief life of light.

Commentary on Art Work and Portfolio

Following are examples of Patrick's paintings preceded by representative quotations from his art school sketch work books and two citations he received.

<u>Leonardo de Vinci</u> – *One of my favorite artists. His drawings are much like my pencil life drawings. In my life drawings I really concentrate on anatomy, proportions and angles. In the summer VCU class I learned a lot about Renaissance techniques. I think these techniques have improved my art more than anything else.*

<u>Kehinde Wiley</u> – *I really like his realistic style and background colors. Realism is the best style of art. His art really relates to my most recent piece* ("Funeral is Over" in Portfolio) *because it has interesting patterns in the background.*

<u>Matt Adams</u> – *His fish on ice paintings inspired me for my next piece* ("Great Catch" in Portfolio). *I paid close attention to the reflections on ice from the fish's red scales. I applied this technique by using my imagination to create a reflection on ice of the red hue on the Coke bottle.*

<u>Robert Longo</u> – *His pieces have a sort of flow in them. The drawings have a lot of contrast but they are still realistic. For this painting* ("Morning Sun" in Portfolio) *I am painting my brother in a dramatic pose just trying to remove his shirt.*

<u>Stylistic Pursuit</u> – Patrick studied the works of many artists with many styles and was in the process of developing his own. He leaned toward realism touched with impressionism.

It is impossible to say what his individual style would have evolved into, but, maybe because of a youthful lack of sophistication, he was not soon headed toward abstract art. Below are three entries in two different sketch workbooks when he was sixteen:

> *Abstract has changed the way I think of art. To me abstract is the basic principle to art. Every time I do a painting I start off abstractly. I then eventually start putting in the details and all the pieces come together to form the painting. Personally I consider 'abstract art,' but I consider it <u>unfinished</u> art. It is art where you have to guess the subject. It is like reading a sentence without a subject, but it has a direct object to give the reader a clue.*

He reports in another entry that he did complete an abstract painting when required to do so by one of his teachers, and punctuates it with his youthful exuberance:

> *Winter break is here! Hurrah. I also finished my abstract project. My abstract piece looks awesome! I have had a great week, PS I found $2 on the ground this morning.*

He continued to wrestle with what he considered honest art:

> *All art should be a certain mystery and should make demands on the spectator. Giving a sculpture or a drawing a too explicit title takes away part of that mystery.* [But] *I do not want to make art that offends others or looks like anything such as abstract. I want to make art that looks like life. I don't want to have to <u>lie</u> about what I created to make it art.*

Certificate of Special Congressional Recognition

Presented to

Patrick Gorman

*in recognition of your participation in
"An Artistic Discovery"
the Congressional Art Competition for High School Students.*

May 8, 2009
DATE

MEMBER OF CONGRESS

National Art Education Association

NATIONAL ART HONOR SOCIETY

Certificate of Membership

certifying that

Patrick Gorman

has been selected as a member of the

2028

chapter of the National Art Honor Society
for High School Students.

Membership is based upon:
Art Scholarship ▪ Character ▪ Service

Principal

Sponsor

4/15/10
Date

A Program of
NAEA

National Art Education Association
www.arteducators.org

Untitled sketch, charcoal

Barn Scene – Painted at age fourteen

Self Portrait – Reflecting "punk" alter ego

Life Orange – Still life

Great Catch – Fish on ice

Funeral is Over – Cousin Hank after his great uncle's funeral

Morning Sun – A portrait of brother, Jack

Breck – Unfinished portrait of his dad

VIRGINIA WILDLIFE

APRIL 2011   FOUR DOLLARS

In this Issue
Journey of the Red Knot
James River Sturgeon
Fly Rod Chronicles

Beautiful Brookie – cover, *Virginia Wildlife* magazine, April 2011